SARATOGA

HEALTH HISTORY HORSES HI-TECH

Saratoga history stretches back to the Mohawks, who credited the area's naturally carbonated mineral springs with healing powers. The Saratoga story continues with the American War for Independence—the Battle of Saratoga in 1777 marked a turning point in the war. By the early 1800s, Saratoga's vaunted waters made it a summer destination for the well-to-do, and in 1863, the new race track turned Saratoga into an international attraction. The huge hotels of the Victorian era became summer haunts for Gilded Age figures like J.P. Morgan and "Diamond Jim" Brady, and 20th-century stars like Bing Crosby and Sophie Tucker played to packed casino and hotel crowds.

Today Saratoga enters its newest phase, with a second international event, the arrival of GLOBALFOUNDRIES and the semiconductor industry.

"Saratoga always tries to stay up with the latest fashions. That is why there are so many distinct styles of architecture over many years. In the world of American architecture it is unrivaled, not only for all the phases of Victorian architecture, but for every period from Colonial to Ranch."
–Harvard and Skidmore Professor James Kettlewell

"...the word 'Saratoga' is known to be a corruption of a Native American place name; authorities disagree on what the exact word was, and hence what it meant."
–From the Saratoga County Chamber of Commerce

"This is a very beautiful part of the world you have here..."
–Marty Balin, Jefferson Airplane, from the stage at the Saratoga Performing Arts Center

"Saratoga is so great that your kids will come back to visit you."
–Father Thomas Park, Bethesda Episcopal Church

Art Direction by Bdesign
Production by Peter and Marjorie Olsen
Archival photos courtesy of the Saratoga Springs History Museum
First Edition

Published by entropic gravity associates
ISBN 978-0-615-51389-8
Library of Congress Control Number: 2011934996

SARATOGA

HEALTH HISTORY HORSES HI-TECH

Snapshots of Saratoga Springs

Circular Street Architecture

The Batcheller Mansion, now operated as a lavish bed & breakfast, is a spectacular example of High-Victorian Gothic Style, framed in solid mahogany.

Batcheller Mansion

The Batcheller was built in 1873 by George Sherman Batcheller, a Civil War general who became a New York State diplomat. Shortly after the house was constructed, he was appointed to Egypt's International Tribunal. Mr. Batcheller spent a great part of his life in Egypt, and rarely resided in the Batcheller Mansion. He was also the first president of the World Bank and an ambassador to Portugal.

Batcheller Mansion

right: Professor Hollis Palmer and Sandra Graff portray George Sherman Batcheller and Catharine Batcheller for historic tours.

below: Dan DelGaudio, the Batcheller's manager and chef, describes the nuances of High-Victorian Tea on Mother's Day.

left: George Sherman Batcheller, circa 1887.

right: Circa 1874.

Circular Street Architecture

Early/High-Victorian Italian Villa Style.

Victorian Italianate.

French Renaissance/Second Empire Style.
Part of the old Skidmore Campus.

Victorian Italianate.

Queen Anne evolving into the Colonial Revival.

Circa 1910.

Circular Street Architecture

A building currently used for social services and offices by a Presbyterian church, in French Renaissance/Second Empire Style with the classic mansard roof. The original iron cresting on top is still intact.

right: Greek Revival Style.

This former Congregational church, now converted to apartments, is a Gothic-Victorian version of the Romanesque Revival.

wo variations on Italian Style.

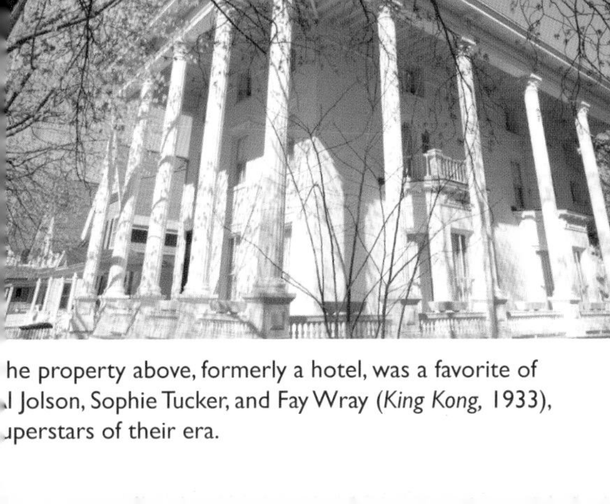

he property above, formerly a hotel, was a favorite of l Jolson, Sophie Tucker, and Fay Wray (*King Kong,* 1933), uperstars of their era.

Circular Street Architecture

below: Madame Jumel's Classic Greek Revival home. She was a consort in Napoleon's court and married Vice President Aaron Burr, who shot and killed Alexander Hamilton in a duel in 1804.

At one point she was the largest landholder in Saratoga Springs. An iconic figure in Saratoga history, she was born out of wedlock to a prostitute, and her mother was jailed when she was ten years old. Madame Jumel's dinner parties included Thomas Jefferson, James Fenimore Cooper, Joseph Bonaparte, and General Lafayette.

A house that has evolved through various phases of nineteenth-century architecture.

Eliza Jumel

Lake Avenue Architecture

A Queen Anne Victorian designed by Saratoga architect Newton Brezee.

R. NEWTON BREZEE,
EXECUTIVE COMMITTEE FETE 1897.
DESIGNS.

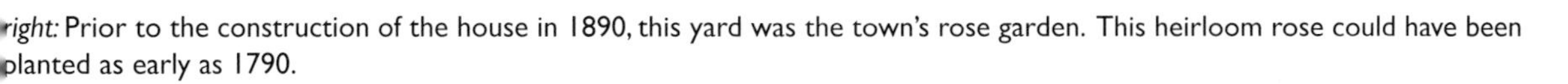

right: Prior to the construction of the house in 1890, this yard was the town's rose garden. This heirloom rose could have been planted as early as 1790.

Caroline Street Architecture

A horse-of-a-different-color on the porch of the Children's Museum.

above: This property is an example of a great Victorian from the 1800s that had fallen in disrepair and needed significant renovation. While the core of the house is original, its contemporary additions have enhanced its architectural qualities.

Behind this large Victorian is a stone stable (*right*), which has been converted to apartments.

Phila Street Architecture

High-Victorian Gothic Style.

Fifth Avenue Architecture

High-Victorian Italianate Style.

Union Avenue Architecture

Queen Anne Style, often with a stone exterior on the first floor.

Colonial Revival. Built by Sam Riddle, the owner of Man O'War and War Admiral, the famous racehorses.

Classic Colonial Revival. Said to have been built by "Diamond Jim" Brady for Lillian Russell.

Related to High-Victorian Gothic, but unique in no particular style.

Classic Queen Anne Style.

Queen Anne Style with Elizabethan/Jacobean influences.

A tour-de-force Queen Anne by S. Gifford Slocum.

Colonial Revival/Beaux-Arts Style.

High-Victorian Gothic.

Late Greek Revival/transition to Italian Style.

North Broadway Architecture

The Brackett House, a Queen Anne Style home owned by Senator Edgar Truman Brackett, the founder of the Adirondack Trust Company and the McGregor Links Golf Course.

According to popular myth, Brackett's wife did not like the sole banker in town. When Brackett told her, "Be nice to him, he owns the only bank," she replied, "Well then, start your own bank."

North Broadway Architecture

Queen Anne/Aesthetic Movement house, created by S. Gifford Slocum. Upstate New York had many craftsmen who produced outstanding terracotta work.

In 1882, Oscar Wilde lectured for two weeks in Saratoga on the Aesthetic Movement.

North Broadway Architecture

Diamond Jim Brady and Lillian Russell's house, adjacent to North Broadway.

Many Saratoga homes are so surrounded by shrubbery that they can only be seen well in winter or early spring.

The red (beaded) mortar joints, clearly visible between the stones, are a signature of architect Henry Hobson Richardson, who was responsible for the Queen Anne/Romanesque Revival Style. Internationally, Richardson is considered the most influential architect of the nineteenth century. Stanford White learned his craft as an assistant to Richardson.

North Broadway Architecture

right: The home of Skidmore College's president. Originally the home of Skidmore founder Lucy Skidmore Scribner, its Queen Anne Style blends with Colonial Revival elements.

Italian Style remodeled in Colonial Revival Style.

Colonial Revival by Alfred Hopkins.

Excelsior Avenue Architecture

High-Victorian Gothic Cottage style. Presently being restored, these three little cottages from 1872 were once the residence of Charles Brackett, son of the banker Edgar Brackett.

Charles was an educator who moved to Los Angeles and became a scriptwriter, receiving Oscars for *Lost Weekend, Sunset Boulevard,* and *Titanic* (1953). He also wrote and produced the screenplays for *Ninotchka* with Garbo, and *Niagara* with Monroe, and collaborated with Billy Wilder on thirteen movies.

he cottage on the left contained his library, which now resides at Skidmore. Out of all the grand buildings in Saratoga, they are the favorite structures of many historians, architects, and preservationists. The buildings were originally constructed by Sarah F. Smiley, one of the first female ministers.

Spring Street Architecture

Early Victorian Gothic, often referred to as Stick Style.

Late Italian Style.

West Side Architecture

French Renaissance/Second Empire row houses, inspired by Parisian row houses.

Classic Greek Revival Style.

A Queen Anne residence near Skidmore, designed by S. Gifford Slocum. Tabloid fodder from the t of the last century: Harry Kendall Thaw, who once lived in this house, was a millionaire whose wif was Evelyn Nesbit, a famous showgirl of the time. In 1906, in a jealous rage over Evelyn, Thaw shot and killed internationally renowned architect Stanford White, a murder that William Randolph He called "The Crime of the Century." (Hearst, being a newspaperman, did call other events "The Cri of the Century," however.)

When a movie of Evelyn's life was made in Hollywood in the 1950s, *The Girl in the Red Velvet Swing*, the scriptwriter was Saratoga's Charles Brackett!

West Side Architecture

A charming Colonial, often referred to as "The Nantucket House."

Classic Greek Revival with a high level of detail work.

Showgirl Evelyn Nesbit and architect Stanford White.

Parts of Saratoga's West Side, with new condos, look like Manhattan's Upper East Side.

Stanford Whites in Saratoga? Three incredible Queen Anne homes, reputedly designed by Stanford White.

Victorian Details

Victorian Doorways

Yaddo

Romanesque Revival Style interpreted by Katrina and Spencer Trask, working with William Halsey Wood in 1891. Yaddo is a not-for-profit artist's community on 400 acres. In 1900 Spencer and Katrina created the plan to turn their estate into this unique corporation dedicated to the arts.

"Its mission is to nurture the creative process by providing an opportunity for artists to work without interruption in a supportive environment."
–Yaddo

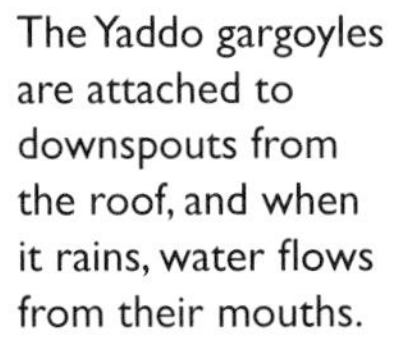

The Yaddo gargoyles are attached to downspouts from the roof, and when it rains, water flows from their mouths.

Artists apply for residencies that last from two weeks to two months and include room, board, and studio.

Visitors to Yaddo have included Saul Bellow, John Cheever, Milton Avery, James Baldwin, Leonard Bernstein, Truman Capote, Aaron Copland, Philip Guston, Patricia Highsmith, Langston Hughes, Henri Cartier-Bresson, and Sylvia Plath.

Yaddo Gardens

The gardens host over 40,000 visitors annually and are maintained by Yaddo buildings and grounds staff and a group of committed, local volunteers.

Yaddo requests that visitors respect the privacy of the artists in residence.

Spencer and Katrina Trask.

Broadway

Saratoga Springs' City Hall, in Classic-Victorian Italianate Style. Shown with original clock tower, circa 1899.

Classic American Diner.

High-Victorian Gothic Influence.

Artist Greg Montgomery creates Saratoga Race Course posters.

Victorian-era apothecary.

Circus Café sells original t-shirts to circus workers worldwide.

Broadway

Uncommon Grounds is a local coffee shop with freshly roasted coffee and a great porch for people watching. Matt Loiacono roasts the Monsooned Malabar.

Summer evenings find motorcycles lined up in front of Uncommon Grounds.

Victorian porches benefit from a good bottle of wine.

"Best Equestrian Themed Shop on the Planet" – *The New York Daily News*

Saratoga is the town that was built by the horse, and Impressions of Saratoga presents items that celebrate the horse and the track.

The "Tree of Giving" supports dozens of local charities.

An assortment of locally made gourmet treats including the famous Saratoga Peppermint Pig ™.

Broadway

Saratoga Springs' Broadway Post Office, built in 1910, was designed by James Knox Taylor, the supervising architect of the United States Treasury.

The original street lamps shown in this 1920s photo are now in front of the Canfield Casino.

High-Victorian/Italianate Influence.

Broadway

Classic Works Progress Admininistration murals, painted in 1937 by Guy Pène du Bois for the Broadway Post Office. Their Saratoga subject matter makes them priceless today.

"The Adelphi Hotel is the grande dame of Saratoga Springs."

– The New York Times

Built in 1877, the Adelphi Hotel is the sole survivor of the great Victorian hotels, and a national treasure. The Adelphi is an Italianate building with a Victorian-Gothic porch. Part of the mystique of the Adelphi is that, like Siro's Restaurant, it is only open for the summer months, catering especially to ballet and track enthusiasts.

Adelphi, circa 1899, with beautiful American elm tees.

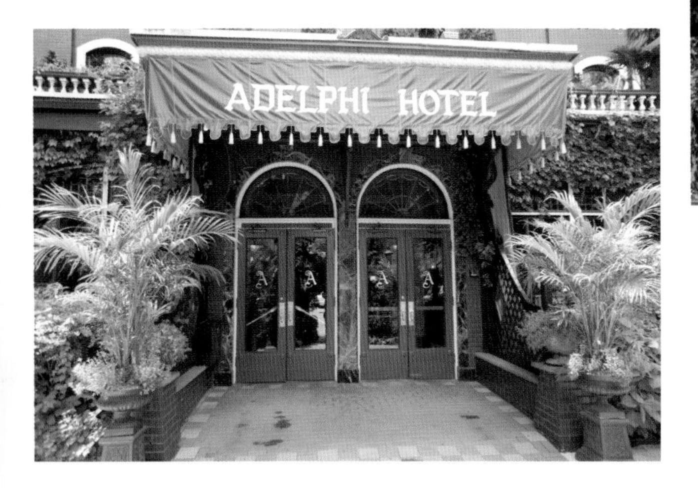

Perhaps more than any other place in Saratoga, the ninety-foot private balcony on the second floor overlooking Broadway takes you back to the town's Gilded Age.

Saratoga titan John Morrissey enjoyed the Adelphi, and passed away in the second floor parlor in 1878.

ach room is magnificently decorated, with Victorian, Adirondack, Colonial, Country French, and Country English themes.

The fourth floor displays the owner's personal collection of American Folk Art.

The rear garden patio and café lounge are open to the public.

The enclosed garden's Beaux-Arts Style pool is available to residents.

The Adirondack Trust Company

The only bank locally owned and operated in Saratoga Springs has been on Broadway since 1901.

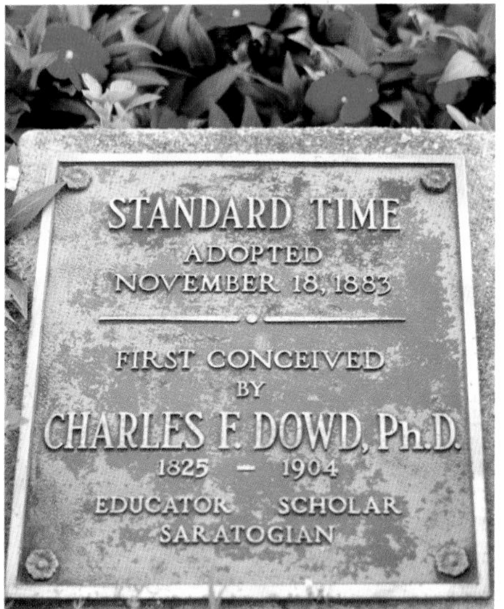

STANDARD TIME
ADOPTED
NOVEMBER 18, 1883
FIRST CONCEIVED
BY
CHARLES F. DOWD, Ph.D.
1825 – 1904
EDUCATOR SCHOLAR
SARATOGIAN

Saratoga educator Charles S. Dowd proposed a system of U.S. time zones, which this sculpture commemorates. His brilliant idea was institutionalized by the U.S. railroad companies.

The Adirondack Trust Company

The bank lobby, built in 1916, was created by American architect Alfred Hopkins, who studied in the French Beaux-Arts School in Paris.

The Adirondack Trust board room displays a remarkable level of craftsmanship in the Colonial Revival Style.

The Saratoga Springs Heritage Area Visitor Center

Housed in a 1915 Beaux-Arts trolley station, the Saratoga Springs Visitor Center not only provides current information to out-of-town guests, but is deeply committed to promoting the cultural, historical, and natural resources of the town and county.

Modern Architecture with Victorian DNA

Congress Park Centre contains shops, office space, and condominiums, and is a post-modern interpretation of traditional Victorian themes. Currently it is the home of Ayco, a leading financial investment firm.

Congress Park Centre was built at the site of the Grand Union Hotel, which was the largest hotel in the world at one time.

Modern Architecture with Victorian DNA

The world's only Victorian McDonald's! Some may say that a Queen Anne Style McDonald's pushes the Victorian theme too far, but it is good fun.

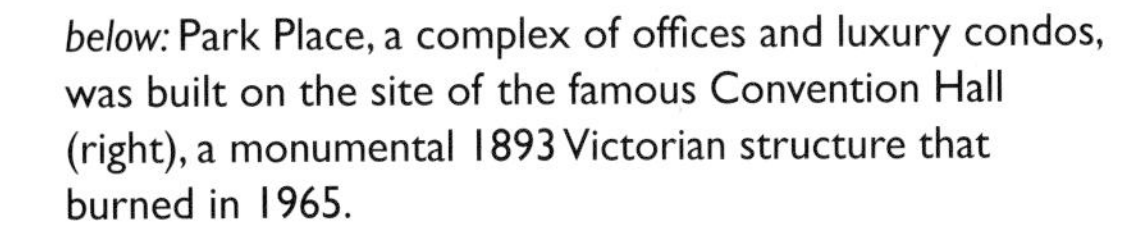

below: Park Place, a complex of offices and luxury condos, was built on the site of the famous Convention Hall (right), a monumental 1893 Victorian structure that burned in 1965.

A technologically advanced facility at Empire State College, the online learning division of the State University of New York. *below:* The Empire State College building was built on the site of the Mabee house, and retains the original stone wall.

A one-of-a-kind Hampton Inn & Suites

Victorian architects would appreciate the porches, angles, and details of this unique Hampton Inn & Suites, with a grand staircase, hardwood floors, chandeliers, and a two-story lobby. Located downtown near Broadway, its parking garage is priceless during track season.

Jacob & Anthony's American Grille boasts a large bar and an outside patio with a fire-pit. The menu features classic recipes of steak and seafood with a modern presentation.

Uniquely styled conference rooms with the latest technology.

The Gut

The "Gut" is only four blocks square, but is home to thirty restaurants, bars, and music establishments. In July and August it is as busy as New Orleans' Bourbon Street, and many venues are open until 4 am.

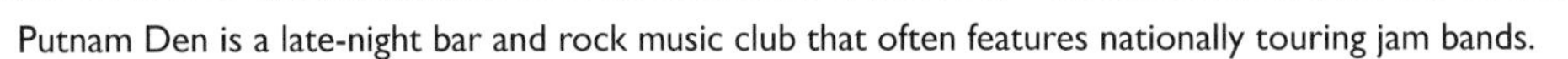

Putnam Den is a late-night bar and rock music club that often features nationally touring jam bands.

At Trotter's you can get horse racing tips from track workers.

The staff at Union Coach Works, which is conveniently located downtown.

Four Seasons Natural Foods.

Ben and Jerry personally designed this store, their first outside of Vermont.

Caroline Street

Trivia: Don McLean wrote "American Pie" in a booth at the Tin & Lint Company.

Caroline Street at 2 am after the Travers Stakes Race.

Caroline Street

One-of-a-kind stores like Saratoga Guitar make shopping downtown an eclectic experience.

Popular with students, Esperanto offers fusion cuisine, very late at night.

Phila Street

Caffè Lena is an icon on the folk circuit. Bob Dylan often slept on the floor between Friday and Saturday shows. Lena's is the oldest continuously operated folk cafe in the nation.

John Hammond is one year shy of his 50th anniversary playing Caffè Lena.

Lyrical Ballad Bookstore is an underground labyrint with antique books, the opposite of big-box stores.

The Algonquin

Romanesque Revival Style by S. Gifford Slocum.

below: The Algonquin with the glow of the modern City Center.

Saratoga Springs City Center

The Saratoga Springs City Center hosts national conventions and recently added two conference centers, enlarging it to more than 30,000 square feet.

Before the Convention Center, Duesenbergs and Rolls Royces were shown in the Crystal Room at the Grand Union Hotel.

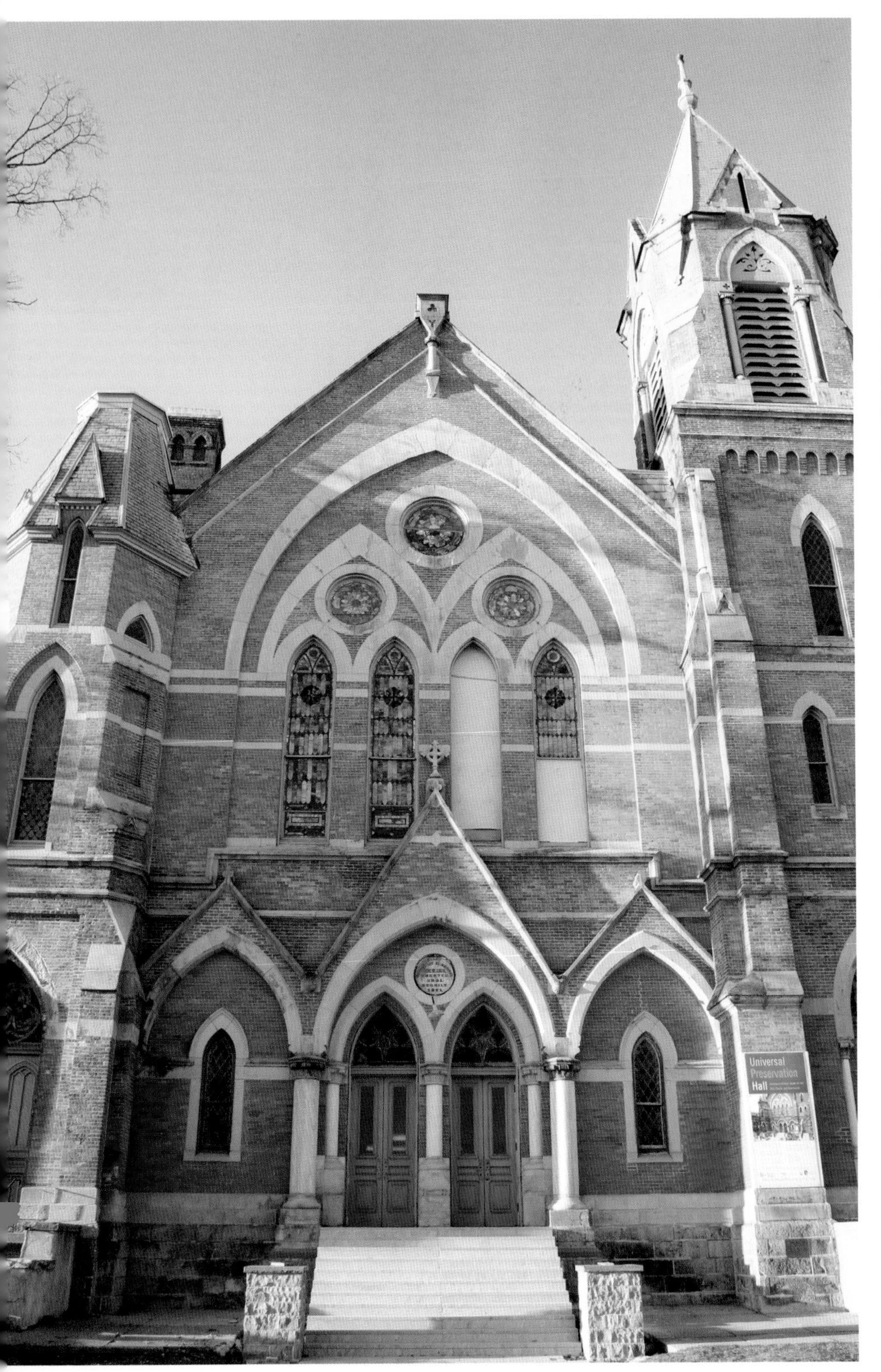

Universal Preservation Hall

Currently being developed as a not-for-profit performing arts center, Universal Preservation Hall was built in 1871 as a Methodist church. Given its beauty, it has the potential to be one of the finest music halls in the Northeast.

Congress Park: The Spirit of Life

The Trask statue by Daniel Chester French, who created the Lincoln Memorial. "The Spirit of Life" is considered to be his masterpiece. Originally he wanted to portray her naked, but Katrina Trask felt clothes would be more appropriate.

Circa 1914.

Congress Park

Designed by Frederick Law Olmsted, at the same time he was creating Central Park in New York City.

The carousel horses were hand carved in 1910.

A free Shakespeare festival is held every summer.

Congress Park: The Italian Garden

In Europe there are many gardens like this, but they are generally not open to the public.

"Spit and Spat" fountains. The sons of Poseidon.

Congress Park: The Canfield Casino

The Canfield Casino, America's first European-style gambling casino, was built in 1870 by John Morrissey, who also founded the thoroughbred track and collegiate rowing races at Saratoga Lake. A champion boxer, Morrissey also served as a Congressman and New York State Senator. Before moving to Saratoga, he lived in New York City where he operated several casinos. Early in his career he achieved notoriety for a fight in a brothel, in which he may have had a business interest.

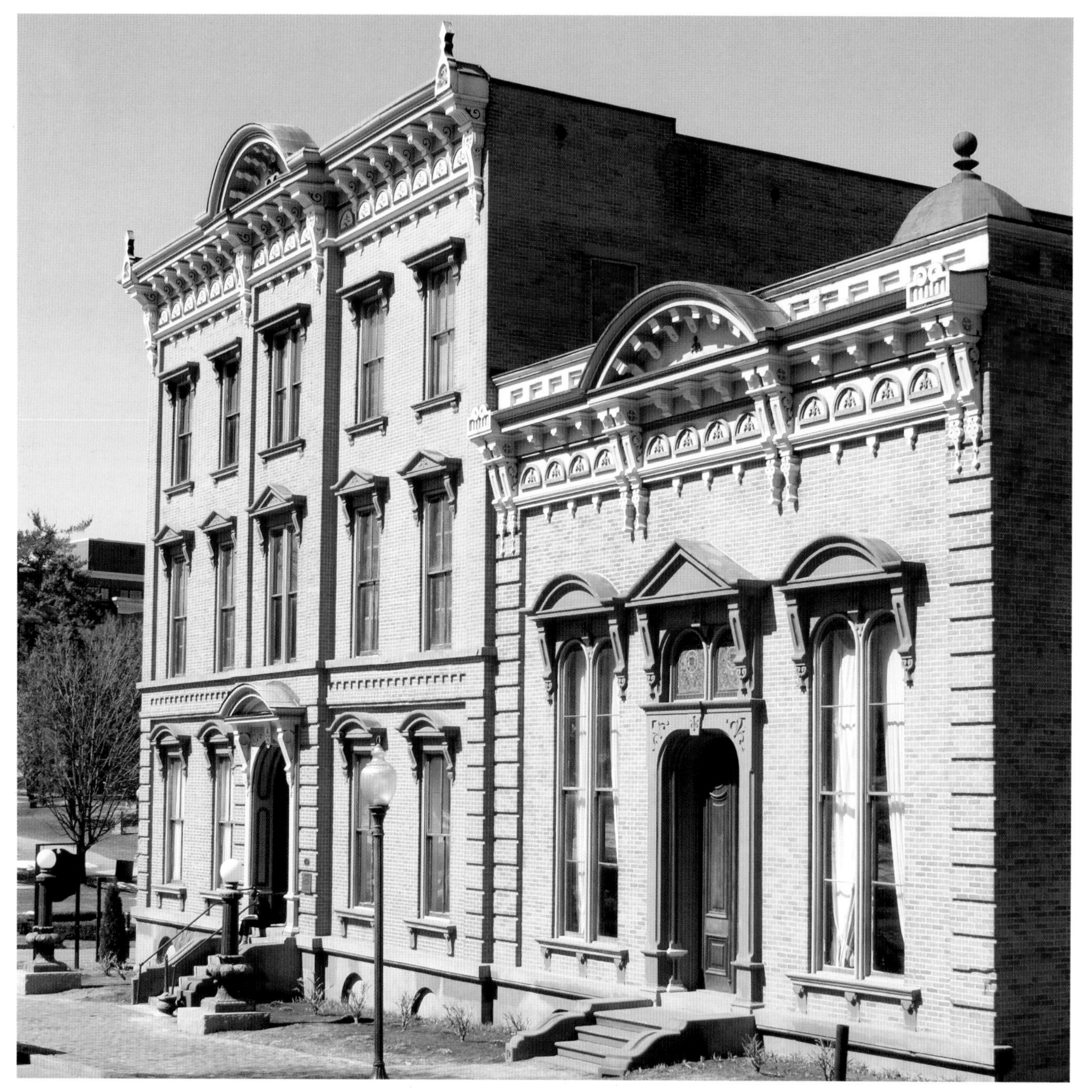

The Canfield Casino's Beaux-Arts Classical ballroom was added by Richard Canfield in 1903. The building is a National Historic Landmark.

Congress Park: The Canfield Casino

The Canfield Casino Parlor

This High-Victorian interior was frequented by "Diamond Jim" Brady, Franklin Roosevelt, Thomas Edison, Will Rogers, Groucho Marx, Oscar Wilde, and Bing Crosby. And of course, local heroes Madame Jumel and Edgar Brackett.

Congress Park: Historical Reenactors

Mohawk descendents in war paint. The Mohawk with the bow is dressed circa 1600, and the Mohawk with the rifle is circa 1700.

Civil War era Fifth New York, Duryee Zouaves.

The ribbon cutting for the new City Center addition.

Saratoga Mayors.

above: A rogues' gallery of past and present downtown restaurant and pub owners.

The color guard at the City Center dedication.

Saratoga Small Town Charm

Saratoga has many great annual events that are organized by the chamber of commerce and local city organizations.

A Halloween Pumpkin Roll down Caroline Street.

Dance Flurry in February brings participants and spectators from around the country.

Carolers at the Victorian Street Walk.

Saratoga's First Night Celebration presents concerts and family-oriented activities at many venues.

> "Saratoga is a little town in big pajamas."
>
> *– Thomas Alexander, fifth-generation Saratogian*

The "Hats Off" Celebration welcomes the return of the race track every July, with a weekend of over a dozen bands performing free throughout the city.

Saratoga Small Town Charm

left: Blues great George Boone tears it up at the annual Saratoga Arts Fest. *below:* Fife & Drum Corps at the Flag Day Parade.

The old grey barns at Allerdice provided the material that literally built the town.

Saratoga High School graduations are held at the Saratoga Performing Arts Center.

below: Racing City Chorus.

Stewart's, a locally based chain of convenience stores, with award-winning ice cream.

Fourth of July Parade

There are many fireworks displays for the Fourth of July, including this one at the Racino. The show in Congress Park has taken place for over 150 years.

Grasso's Italian Ices

When people in Manhattan hear "Saratoga" they think of horse racing in the summer. When people raised in Saratoga think of summer, one of the first thoughts is often Grasso's.

Bethesda Episcopal Church

One of the first Gothic Revival churches in the country, with sublime Tiffany windows.

Louis Comfort Tiffany, a friend of the Trask family of Saratoga, created these stained-glass angels at their request.

"Katrina Trask was so bereaved by the death of her husband Spencer that she could not attend the service at the Bethesda Church."

–Lesley Leduc, Yaddo

Muse Architect

"Saratoga Springs is a three-dimensional library of the history of American architecture. I reference and enjoy the classic buildings and they have a great impact on my architectural work. The collective beauty of this city enriches my life daily."
–John Muse

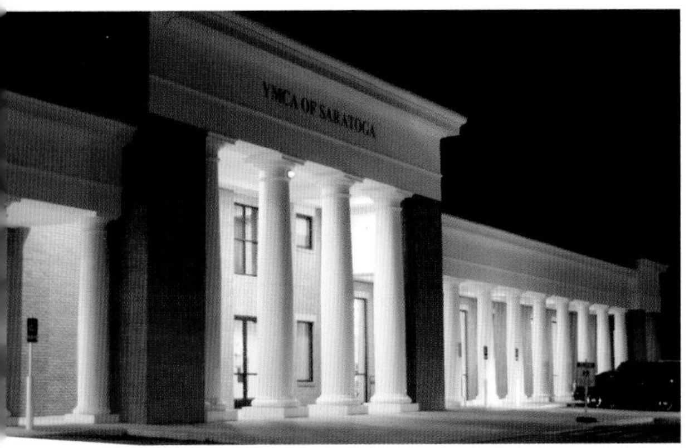

The Muse projects displayed on this page have roots in the historic architectural fabric of the city, while being original in their own right.

Essential Community Services

Not all in Saratoga drive Porsches and drink Pétrus. Support agencies like the Economic Opportunity Council (EOC) soup kitchen, Hospice, Meals On Wheels, Elder Services, ASPCA, and many more, help keep the town a decent place to live.

Julie Hoxie, the EOC's Executive Director, helps provide community services, energy services, Head Start, Latino Community Advocacy Program, and Wheels for Work.

Shelters of Saratoga provides housing assistance.

Kari Cushing, Executive Director, and Bo Goliber, Coordinator of Development & Volunteers, organize the pantry at the Franklin Community Center, which offers a food pantry, distribution center, holiday assistance, and back-to-school assistance, as well as Project Lift. They accept food donations directly from the community.

Farmers Market

The Farmers Market is foodie heaven, and provides fresh and organic veggies, as well as homemade bread, cheeses, and condiments.

During the summer there are as many as fifty vendors, and the American Farmland Trust voted the Saratoga Farmers Market the third best in the nation.

The Saratoga Race Course

Celebrating its 150th anniversary in 2013, the Saratoga Springs Race Course is the oldest operating race track in the country. It even ran during the Civil War.

Sam the bugler.

The Saratoga Race Course

Filly Rachel Alexandra beats the boys with jockey Calvin Burrell. Owner Jess Jackson, of Kendall-Jackson Wines, smiles.

The Saratoga Race Course

Queen Anne/Romanesque Style; rebuilt in 1902. More than 40,000 fans attend on Travers Day.

The Saratoga Race Course

Summer Bird, owned by Marylou Whitney, wins the Travers.

below: Christianne Smith in a dress by Tom and Linda Platt. The horses appreciate it when you dress up for the track.

The Travers Cup.

The Oklahoma Track is next to the Saratoga Race Course and is used for training and practice. Horse Haven, the location of the original track, founded by John Morrissey in 1863, was just south of the Oklahoma Track. Racing in Saratoga initially started downtown on Friday and Saturday nights, when groups of people would unofficially organize races on a loop around Broadway! It became so popular (and dangerous) that the need for a formal track was obvious, and racing started at Horse Haven.

2

Fasig-Tipton

Need to auction a three-million-dollar horse?

Saratoga is a stable community.

Saratoga Polo at the Whitney Field

Established in 1898, the Saratoga Polo Club meets are held from July 8 through Labor Day.

Marylou Whitney and Charlie Hayward

Philanthropist, businesswoman, horse owner, and reigning Queen of Saratoga, Marylou's love of the town is legendary. Mr. Hayward is the President of the New York Racing Association.

McMahon Thoroughbred Farm

The home of Funnycide.

The Harness Track

Saratoga Automobile Museum

At home in a former mineral water bottling-plant, the Saratoga Automobile Museum changes its exhibits three times annually.

A five-million-dollar Alfa Romeo.

Guest lecturer
and board member.

How Charles Lindbergh got around on the ground.

A 1935 Maserati named Poison Lil.

The National Museum of Dance

The museum occupies the former Washington Bath House, a 1919 Arts & Crafts building.

Necklace
This necklace is made up of both Native manufactured (bird bone tubular beads, drilled animal teeth, kettle brass tubular beads) and European manufactured trade beads.

The Saratoga Springs History Museum

Located in the Canfield Casino in Congress Park since 1911. The Saratoga Historical Society was founded in 1883 and was one of the earliest organizations of its type.

A Tiffany window from Mr. Canfield's office.

The New York State Military Museum

This Romanesque Revival Style building was originally an armory, built in 1889.

The National Museum of Racing

The museum was founded in 1950. As of 2011, its Official National Thoroughbred Racing Hall of Fame includes 186 thoroughbreds, 93 jockeys, and 88 trainers.

Beekman Street Arts District

Small, independent art galleries and restaurants on Saratoga's West Side add to the town's vibrancy.

The Congress Hotel once occupied the Saratoga Arts Center's site.

The Saratoga Arts Center

Not-for-profit Saratoga Arts presents art exhibits, art classes and workshops, a variety of performances, and cinema with the Saratoga Film Forum.

The Saratoga Performing Arts Center

The Saratoga Performing Arts Center opened in July 1966; SPAC founder Robert McKelvey cut the ribbon. The roofed amphitheater seats 5,200. The all-time attendance record was set June 27, 1985 by the Grateful Dead, with 40,231 in attendance.

Concerts at the Saratoga Performing Arts Center

above: Levon Helm Band.

left: Bob Dylan.

above: Sir Elton John.

above: The Kings of Leon.
below: Peter Gabriel and the New Blood Orchestra.

Phish.

Bob Weir from the Grateful Dead, performing with Further.

The Al Green Show.

Forty years of the Allman Brothers Band.

Jerry Garcia of the Grateful Dead, in 1977.

Before the Philadelphia Orchestra, Saratogians enjoyed the 60-piece Grand Union Hotel Band (above, circa 1899).

SPAC presents the Freihofer's Jazz Festival

The Freihofer's Jazz Festival, now in its thirty-fourth year, attacts fans from around the country for a weekend of music every June.

A great idea: Many families use the jazz festival as an occasion for an annual family reunion. Relatives travel to Saratoga to get together for a Saturday and Sunday of picnics and over thirty bands.

The Philadelphia Orchestra

The Philadelphia Orchestra often presents guest artists, with past performers including Yo-Yo Ma, Itzhak Perlman, and André Watts. Typically they perform in August for three weeks, following the ballet residency.

The New York City Ballet

This world-class troupe has been a special part of SPAC from its inception. There are other performing arts centers in the Northeast, but none with this residency. Saratogian Robert McKelvey is credited with the negotiations to bring the New York City Ballet to SPAC.

Saratoga Wine & Food and Fall Ferrari Festival

On a September weekend a hundred Ferraris and thousands of wines descend upon the Saratoga Performing Arts Center for a fund-raising event for the not-for-profit organization.

Renowned wine critic Kevin Zraly leads informative and entertaining seminars.

The Annual Saratoga Automobile Museum Car Show

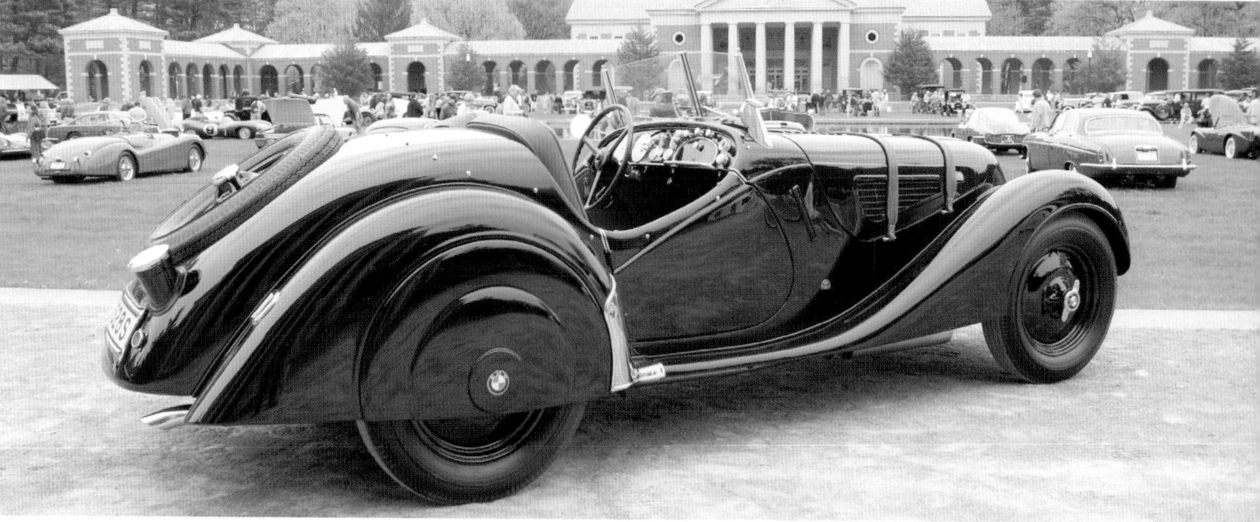

Mrs. Taylor in her D-Jag.

Saratoga Spa State Park

The Saratoga Spa State Park provides 2,400 acres of woods, rivers, trails, geysers, and mineral springs. Most of the historic buildings were built during the Depression by the Works Progress Administration.

Saratoga Spa State Park

In the pediment, Athena, the goddess of wisdom, introduces Asclepius, the god of healing, to a female figure representing Saratoga Springs.

Instrumental in creating the park, Franklin Delano Roosevelt visits Saratoga in 1931.

Saratoga State Park also has Geyser Creek, a trout stream, flowing through the middle!

The Victoria and Peerless Pools in Saratoga Spa State Park

The Victoria Pool complex was designed by Dwight James Baum, working under Joesph Freidlander, the chief architect for the entire Saratoga Spa State Park. Considered a pinnacle of WPA architecture, this beautiful swimming pool is regarded as a late-1930s "last cry" of the Beaux-Arts movement.

Historian James Kettlewell, who consults with the Saratoga Spa State Park, fondly calls the Olympic-size Peerless Pool "Rockefeller Administration-Soviet Style."

Spa Golf in the State Park

In the middle of this well-designed park is a public eighteen-hole golf course that was rated "Four Stars" by *Golf Digest's* "Best Places to Play." Golf fans from around the world are very enthusiastic about the reasonable fees.

The Saratoga Dog Park

A particularly intense game of stick.

The Gideon Putnam Hotel in Spa State Park

The Gideon Putnam Hotel was built in the Saratoga Spa State Park by WPA workers during the 1930s. From here, it's an easy, two-minute walk to the Saratoga Performing Arts Center and the Saratoga Spa Golf Course.

The Gideon Putnam Hotel in Spa State Park

A popular destination for conventions, weddings, and corporate parties.

Roosevelt Baths & Spa

First opened in 1935, the Roosevelt Baths & Spa was recently included in a listing of the "Top 10 New York State Green Destinations" and offers mineral baths, massages, and a range of other services.

The Roosevelt Baths blend their historic charm with modern accents.

The relaxation room.

Hall of Springs, Saratoga Spa State Park

When first constructed, the Hall of Springs complex of buildings contained three mineral springs.

Former President Clinton at a 2011 political rally in the park.

Saratoga Mineral Springs

"Saratoga has become a synonym of 'Health.' And perfect health means perfect happiness. If you want a sound mind, a clear brain, a strong heart, a vigorous body, then pass a portion of each year at Saratoga."

–from *Souvenir Views of Saratoga,*
by Lyman H. Nelson Co. 1899.

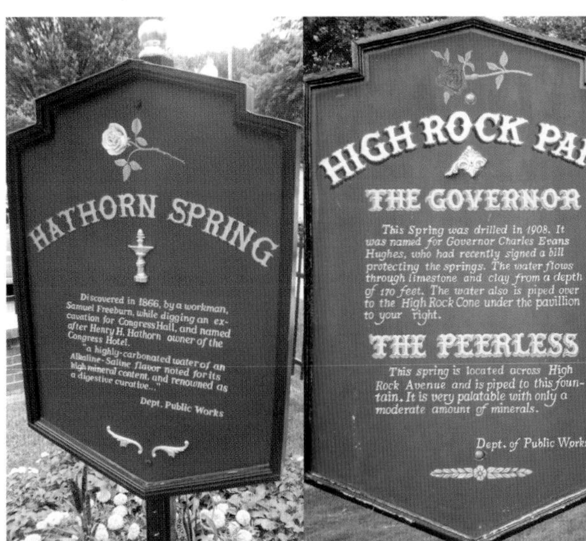

Saratoga Mineral Springs

There are seventeen public mineral springs spread out through town in roughly a north/south line, and many are in the park.

Hayes Spring has a fixture for breathing the carbonated gas from the spring.

Orenda, Hathorn No. 3, and Hayes Spring have very high mineral content.

left: Charlie Spring near the Hall of Springs entrance to SPAC. *above:* The "Spouter" in Geyser Creek.

An Indian Prayer
OH, FATHER, WHOSE VOICE I HEAR IN THE WINDS AND WHOSE BREATH GIVES LIFE TO ALL THE WORLD, HEAR ME. I AM A MAN BEFORE YOU, ONE OF YOUR MANY CHILDREN. I AM SMALL AND WEAK. I NEED YOUR STRENGTH AND WISDOM. LET ME WALK IN BEAUTY, AND MAKE MY EYES EVER BEHOLD THE RED AND PURPLE SUNSET. MAKE MY HANDS RESPECT THE THINGS YOU HAVE MADE, MY EARS SHARP TO HEAR YOUR VOICE. MAKE ME WISE, SO THAT I MAY KNOW THE THINGS YOU HAVE TAUGHT MY PEOPLE, THE LESSONS YOU HAVE HIDDEN IN EVERY LEAF AND ROCK. I SEEK STRENGTH, FATHER--NOT TO BE SUPERIOR TO MY BROTHERS, BUT TO BE ABLE TO FIGHT MY GREATEST ENEMY, MYSELF. MAKE ME EVER READY TO COME TO YOU WITH CLEAN HANDS AND STRAIGHT EYE SO THAT WHEN LIFE FADES AS THE FADING SUNSET, MY SPIRIT MAY COME TO YOU WITHOUT SHAME.
— Tom Whitecloud
DEDICATED BY
INTERESTED CITIZENS OF SARATOGA SPRINGS
1967
THE BICENTENNIAL OF SIR WILLIAM JOHNSON'S VISIT TO HIGH ROCK SPRING

Saratoga Mineral Springs

Europeans started exploring the region in the 1500s, but Native Americans, who greatly valued the springs, were here for thousands of years.

One source notes that while the Mohawks and Mohicans often fought, they were in agreement not to tell the European visitors about the springs. Finally, during a battle in the Revolutionary War, Colonial officer William Johnson was injured at the Battle of Lake George, and Native Americans friendly to the officer brought him to a spring to save his life.

SIR WILLIAM JOHNSON FIRST WHITE MAN
TO PARTAKE OF THE HEALTH GIVING WATERS

THE · FIRST · INHABITANTS
THESE · FOUNTAINS · KNEW
AND · USED · FOR · THEIR
VIRTUES · HIGHLY · PRIZED

George Washington traveled to Saratoga in 1783, and there are drawings of his party camping next to High Rock Spring. He tried to purchase the spring, but the owner refused to sell. The story appeared in newspapers nationally, and greatly popularized Saratoga Springs.

Due to their immense popularity, and the practice of extracting carbonic-acid gas from vast quantities of the water, the springs started to run dry at the turn of the last century. In 1908, the community and state government took action to turn a large tract of land into a health resort, the Spa State Park, and conserve the natural resource.

City Hall mural by Hud Armstrong.

Saratoga Mineral Springs

Big Red Spring is located within the grounds of the Saratoga Race Course.

Anchors of the Community

from top: The YMCA, Saratoga Springs Public Library, Saratoga Springs High School, and the Saratoga Hospital.

The United States Naval Nuclear Power Training Unit

A quiet member of the Saratoga community since the 1950s, the U.S. Naval Nuclear Power Training Unit instructs sailors in submarine and aircraft carrier power-plant operations. The facility is understandably not open to the public.

Skidmore College

Founded in 1903, Skidmore College is a highly selective liberal arts college with approximately 2,400 students and 850 employees. It is also an important community resource for educational programs, cultural activities, entertainment, and volunteer service.

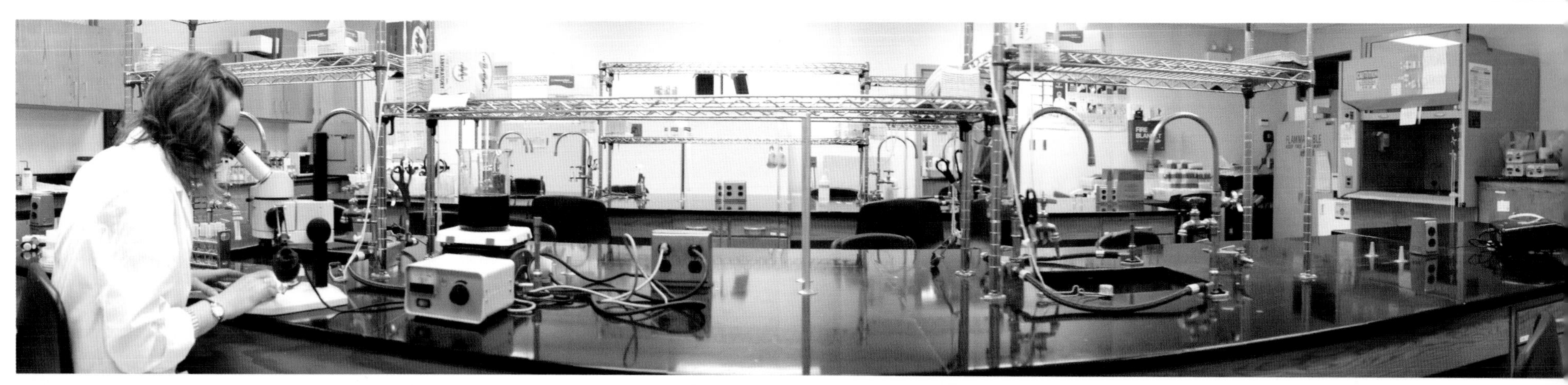

left: Dana Science Center

Skidmore transitioned to the present 850-acre campus on North Broadway starting in the mid-1960s.

'he Arthur Zankel Music Center.

Skidmore started as the Young Women's Industrial Club in 1903.

A graduation on Regent Street in 1933.

The school grew into a complex of buildings on Saratoga's historic East Side.

Skidmore College

Skidmore draws students from over forty states and twenty countries, and nearly sixty percent of the students study abroad.

Skidmore's Frances Young Tang Teaching Museum and Art Gallery is nationally acclaimed for its cross-disciplinary shows.

Saratoga Apple

Ten miles east of downtown, Saratoga Apple has acres of apples, local farm-made cheese, apple cider, store-made cider doughnuts, and often a reggae band on the weekends. Their "u-pick " operation is a popular family destination in the fall.

Owner Nate Darrow grows over a dozen varieties of apples.

BEES POLLENIZE BLOSSOMS
APPLY ROCK DUST SEA SALT & MINERALS

With all-weather greenhouses, organic produce is available year round.

The Parting Glass

The Parting Glass wins national awards from Guinness, and is considered the "Irish Embassy" to Upstate New York.

How good are the McKrells? They regularly tour Ireland.

St. Patrick's Day lunch in the parking lot.

Hometown-hero Commander Cody.

Siro's

A restaurant, bar, and entertainment venue just past the west gate of the track. Siro's is open only during track season and the Kentucky Derby.

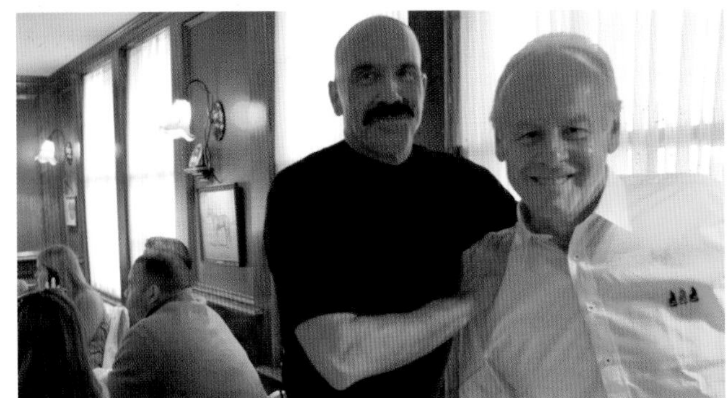

left: Siro's co-owner Paul Carlucci, publisher of the *New York Post*, with Manager Michael Stone (also below).

Chef Tom Dillon: Twenty years of impeccable cuisine.

Max London's Restaurant & Bar

Mediterranean influences with the freshest local produce. This chef-run establishment delivers in-house cheese, bread, and smoked meats with a passionate dedication. The popular weekend brunch runs year round.

A Saturday night jazz jam with no cover and Gene Garone on drums

Mrs. London's

Mrs. London's "is possibly the country's most fabulous bakeshop."
–Food & Wine

"Out-of-towners who think Saratoga Springs is famous for its race track, ballet, sparkling water, and symphony are aware of only four-fifths of the story. There is a landmark here known as Mrs. London's..."
–Craig Claiborne, New York Times

"America's greatest baker."
–Saveur

"[George Balanchine] doesn't want to talk ballet, and all he dreams about from July to July are these confections."
–Craig Claiborne, New York Times

The Olde Bryan Inn

Built in 1826, the inn is constructed on the site of a log cabin that was the first building in Saratoga. The restaurant has maintained the original architecture beautifully, with three working fireplaces. As a locally owned establishment, the Olde Bryan Inn is highly regarded for its involvement in the community.

Longfellows Hotel, Restaurant, and Conference Center

The Twin Barns near Saratoga Lake housed the Saratoga Dairy Farm for close to a century. They are now home to Longfellows, a Saratoga tradition. Longfellows' operations include a restaurant, hotel, bar, conference facilities, banquets, and off-site catering. In the vast and generous Saratoga restaurant community, Longfellows is perhaps the most committed to supporting the Saratoga region and its many residents and not-for-profit organizations.

aratoga has become a national wedding destination, and ongfellows is one of the most popular.

Cafe Capriccio of Saratoga

Capriccio Saratoga opened for the track season in 2011, serving authentic Neapolitan cuisine with, as co-owner Henry Ciccone says, "a Saratoga flair." The first Cafe Capriccio in Albany, NY, is a perennial "readers' poll" winner. The opening of this new trattoria in Saratoga Springs suggests the exciting momentum being generated by the arrival of the semiconductor industry.

Sperry's Restaurant

A fine-dining landmark since 1932, when it began as a speakeasy.
left: Christel and Colin MacLean, co-owners.

above left:
Chef Dale Miller. One of 61 U.S. Certified Master Chefs and one of 300 Global Master Chefs worldwide.

One Caroline Street Bistro

Fifteen years of great music and innovative, farm-fresh food.

The Mouzon House

Committed to high-quality organic vegetables and free-range meat, Mouzon House supports a network of local farms.

A charming Victorian building with outdoor dining and music in the spring, summer, and fall.

PJ's BAR-B-QSA

In business since 1975, PJ's BAR-B-QSA is an authentic Taste Tour of American Barbeque. When rock & roll legend Chuck Berry wants ribs after a show at SPAC, he comes to PJ's. *right:* Their signature drink, PJ's Crystal Beach Loganberry.

Note the classic smoke ring on the brisket, from 13 hours of smoking low and slow.

PJ's turns out Texas brisket, Carolina pulled pork, and Kansas City an Memphis style ribs. *below:* PJ, Carolyn, and Johnny at the outdoor pit.

Hattie's Restaurant

Under the direction of Chef-owner Jasper Alexander, Hattie's Chicken bested Food Network Chef Bobby Flay in a televised chicken "Throwdown!"

Hattie Grey, from St. Francisville, Louisiana, opened the restaurant in 1938. For many years, Hattie's, Lena's and Beverly's were three great enterprises owned and operated by remarkable women on the same street.

Saratoga was fast, man; it was real fast. It was up all night long." *–Hattie on Saratoga in the '30s and '40s.*

The Olde Saratoga Brewery

It's not just a brewpub, it's a full-scale brewery, the fourth largest in New York. Besides award-winning lagers and ales, the Olde Saratoga brews all the Kingfisher Lager sold in the U.S., and all the Mendocino Brewing Company beverages sold in the eastern U.S. A *New York Times* judges' panel recently called Olde Saratoga's Blackhawk Stout the best in America. Saratoga Lager won the Silver Medal at the Great American Beer Festival.

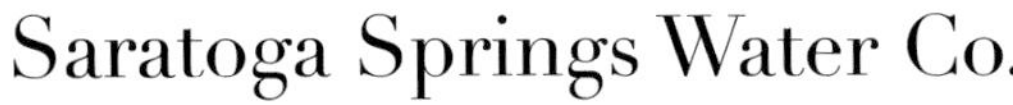

Saratoga Springs Water Co.

Started in 1872 as a family business, the Saratoga Springs Water Co. bottles both still and sparkling water from its famous spring. Originally named "Saratoga Vichy."

Saratoga, "The Queen of American Spas"

In addition to the famous mineral baths and spas, the depth of Saratoga's yoga, meditation, and holistic health community far exceeds its small-town size.

ıe Saratoga Springs Yoga Studio.

Tai-Chi in the park.

McGregor Links Country Club

A championship course open to the public. The course was designed by Devereux Emmet and opened in 1921. The club delivers an incredible 18-hole golf course with a very convenient location.

Circa 1946.

In addition to golf, McGregor Links Country Club offers fine dining, social events, and swimming.

...ydeross Park circa 1922.

A trolley ran from the Grand Union Hotel to Saratoga Lake, circa 1900.

Saratoga Lake / Saratoga Rowing Association

Fish Creek, which feeds the lake, is the practice area for the Saratoga Rowing Association, which has sponsored the national championship at the site. SRA has won nineteen U.S. and Canadian National Championships in the past fifteen years! Since its start, the association has enabled 106 students to receive scholarships to top Division One schools, due in part to the dedication of founder Chris Chase and coach Eric Catalano.

Grant's Cottage

President and General Ulysses S. Grant stayed in this cottage, which is now a national monument, a few miles north of Saratoga and only a few miles from the Hudson River. In June and July of 1895, Grant came here to write his memoirs prior to dying in his bed. His memoirs went on to become a popular best-seller. Remarkably, nothing in the house has been changed since the day he died.

"When people ask, 'How important was Saratoga in the 1800s?' it is important to remember that for the Fourth of July, 1865, General Grant and all of his generals from the Union Army chose to meet in Saratoga. This was three months after Lee surrendered, and the president had been assassinated. They came to celebrate Independence Day and the rebirth of the Union."

– Professor and historian Hollis Palmer, Ph.D.

Miss Carlotta entertained Saratogians with daring balloon flights in Congress Park. Circa 1885.

The Adirondack Balloon Festival

Now in its thirty-seventh year, the Adirondack Balloon Festival, located in nearby Glens Falls, is the largest hot air balloon festival in New York State. Held on a weekend in September, it attracts balloon enthusiasts from around the world with hundreds of balloon flights.

Spectacular Fall Foliage

Saratoga Battlefield

The Battle of Saratoga was the turning point in the Revolutionary War.

"The forces of the Crown surrendered on October 17, 1777. An army of amateurs had defeated a world power." *–From a memorial at the battlefield.*

The General Philip Schuyler House.

Washington County

Washington County sits between Saratoga and Vermont. With beautiful rolling hills, antique shops, artist's galleries, and many family farms, it is a worthwhile day trip.

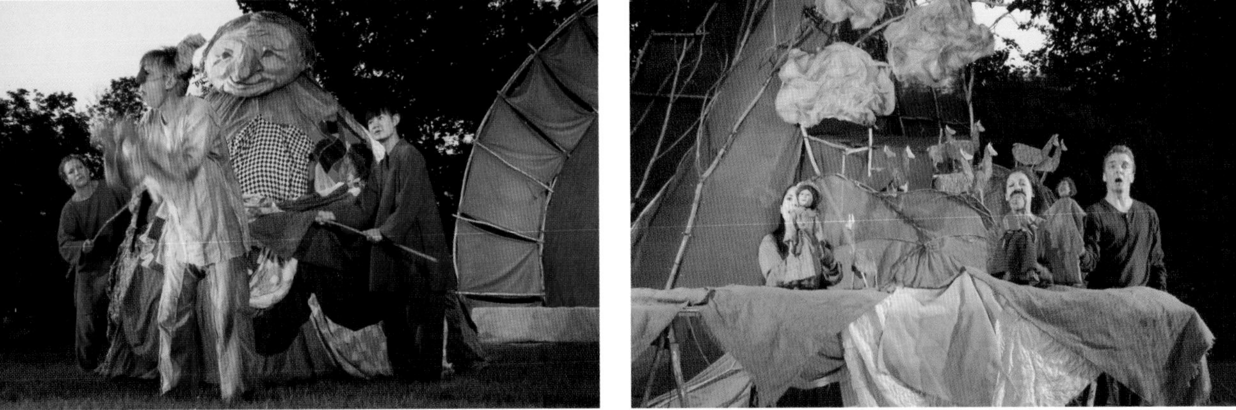

The Mettawee River Company presents a free play every year, and performs in many Washington County locations.

Tour of the Battenkill

The Tour of the Battenkill is the largest one-day race in the United States. This grueling 120-mile race course includes a mix of paved, gravel, and dirt roads, and draws racers from around the world.

The Battenkill River

Flowing out of Vermont's Green Mountains into the Hudson, the Battenkill River is one of the most famous American trout streams. Thomas Jefferson called it "The Queen of American Rivers."

The Adirondack Park

Starting twenty miles north of Saratoga Springs, the park is larger than Yellowstone, Yosemite, Glacier, and the Grand Canyon combined!

Blue Mountain Lake

In the heart of the Adirondacks, Blue Mountain Lake is a beautiful ninety-mile drive from Saratoga Springs.

Lake George

This thirty-mile-long lake at the southern end of the Adirondack Park has many miles of undeveloped shoreline.

Lake George

The lake is so clear that sunken boats from the Revolutionary War attract scuba divers.

Black Mountain Summit

This view from the the peak of Black Mountain, looking north, shows just ten miles of Lake George's thirty-mile stretch.
(To the right is Vermont.) Also visible are some of the Narrow Islands, which have public campsites managed by the New York State Park Service.

left: Buck Mountain is also a top day hike in the Southern Adirondacks, and only forty miles from Saratoga Springs.

The Sagamore Resort at Lake George

The Sagamore has accommodated guests for over a century. It is located on a private island, with a golf course, spa, and nineteenth-century touring boat.

Whiteface Mountain.

Skiing near Saratoga

Saratoga provides many choices for skiing. Whiteface Mountain hosted the 1936 and 1984 Olympics. Many of the leading Vermont resorts are within an hour-and-a-half drive from Saratoga as well. Willard Mountain is fifteen miles from Saratoga Springs.

Gore Mountain, the closest large ski area, is only forty-five miles away.

Willard and West Mountains are great places for kids to learn to ski.

Whiteface Mountain.

The Ausable River near Whiteface

Brown trout and Palen "Catch & Release" Conway. A Saratoga businessman, avid fly-fisherman, and Skidmore graduate, Palen has fished the Ausable since he was five.

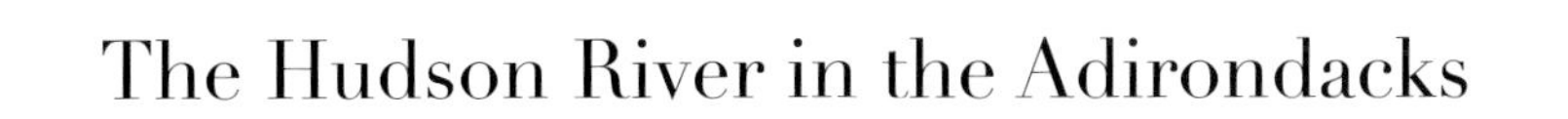

Can you really swim in the Hudson River? You can here.

Quoth the Raven

Some literary events happened in Saratoga outside the sphere of Yaddo.

In the 1840s, Edgar Allan Poe wrote the first draft of the *Raven* when he stayed at the Barhydt's Lake Guest Tavern. Sadly the tavern is long gone, and the lake presently resides within the perimeter of Yaddo (not one of the ponds visible from the road), so it cannot be visited on a literary pilgrimage.

The tavern provided beds, meals, and libations. It is documented that Poe sent his draft from Saratoga to his editor in London.

"While I nodded, nearly napping, suddenly there came a tapping,
As of some one gently rapping, rapping at my chamber door

"Deep into that darkness peering, long I stood there wondering, fearing,
Doubting, dreaming dreams no mortals ever dared to dream before;

"What this grim, ungainly, ghastly, gaunt and ominous bird of yore
Meant in croaking "Nevermore."
–The Raven by Edgar Allan Poe

left: 50th-generation descendent of Poe's Raven?

James Bond in Saratoga

Ian Fleming visited Saratoga on numerous occasions, and in *Diamonds Are Forever* James Bond drives to Saratoga at 100 miles per hour, dines at a possible landmark or two, attends a glitzy horse auction, wins brilliantly at the track, and gets mugged in a health spa!
The book offer scathing insights into gambling, the crime element, and the local government of Saratoga in the 1950s.

"But it was a beautiful day and Bond enjoyed absorbing the Saratoga scene: the milling crowds, the elegance of the owners and their friends in the tree-shaded paddock...the trouble free starts through the tractor-drawn starting gate, the toy lake with its six swans and the anchored canoe…"

"The village of Saratoga Springs...was the Coney Island of the underworld...the mobs exercised dominion over Saratoga for a long time. It was a colony of the national gangs and they ran it with pistols and baseball bats."

"Saratoga seceded from the union as did the other gambling hamlets that placed their municipal governments in the custody of the racket corporations."

"...Bond settled back and silently enjoyed one of the most beautifully landscaped highways in the world and wondered idly what the girl was doing and how, after Saratoga, he was going to get to see her again."

Diamonds Are Forever by Ian Fleming, 1956, the MacMillan Company.

The *Saratogian*

The hometown paper since 1855, the *Saratogian* has exceeded the scope of most small-town papers in part due to its coverage of a yearly international event, the Saratoga Race Course. The *Saratogian* now covers a second international event, the arrival of GLOBALFOUNDRIES.

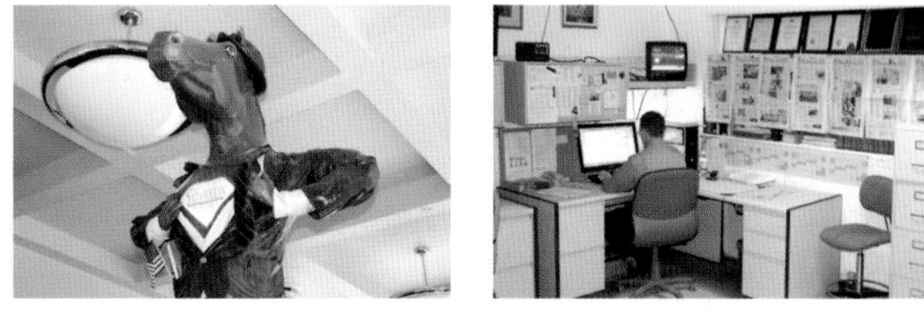

ESPEY Manufacturing & Electronics Corporation

Saratoga's original tech company! Espey is a leader in quality electronic products. Since 1902 this facility has privately produced key parts for the military and military contractors, including General Electric. A publicly traded company since the 1950s.

Momentive Performance Materials Inc.

Momentive Performance Materials Inc. is a global leader in the silicones industry, with a more-than-70-year heritage of innovation and a remarkable history of many industry firsts.

From automotive to healthcare, from electronics to construction, Momentive's silicone materials, specialty products, and enabling technologies are at the frontline of innovation.

Momentive creates custom technology platforms and provides science-based solutions to help its customers increase performance, solve product development issues, and engineer better manufacturing processes.

Momentive attracts top chemists and engineers to Saratoga and the Capital Region. The silicones manufacturer traces its roots in Saratoga County back to GE Silicones, which pioneered the industry.

In addition to its own product line, Momentive makes products branded for GE.

The Radiant Store

The Radiant Store is a leading alternative energy provider in the Northeast. The company specializes in both solar-thermal-heating and solar-photovoltaic systems for both residential and commercial applications.

The Radiant Store creates, installs, and maintains systems with the latest solar technology, and is a licensed partner with Velux and Weismann, two leading European equipment manufacturers.

FMT

Flow Management Technologies re-engineers business processes into profitable businesses. FMT also creates specialized work-flow systems that boost customer responsiveness and employee efficiency, and operates service businesses in the healthcare and banking industries.

Founder & CEO Craig Skevington.

Servers and IT services.

24/7 call center.

C9

C9 may be the smallest semiconductor manufacturer in the Luther Forest Tech Campus, with only seven employees and four robots, but they conduct R&D for the U.S. military, and make silicon graphite composites for missiles and jets. C9 owns four major patents in the semiconductor industry, and part-owner Kevin Donegan individually retains 17 patents.

An advanced atomic layer deposition tool.

Luther Forest Technology Campus

Rapidly becoming a leading international center for the semiconductor industry, Luther Forest Technology Campus offers many ignificant advantages.

This world-class technology campus is the result of a partnership between Luther Forest Technology Campus, Saratoga County Board of Supervisors, Saratoga Economic Development Corporation, and New York State. Located near leading industry resources and erved by a highly skilled technology workforce, the campus is a premier global center for technology leaders.

The 1,414-acre campus delivers the water, electric, gas, telecom, and logistics required by the semiconductor industry.

M+W Group

Known for delivering the world's most technologically advanced facilities, and covering the spectrum of design, construction, and facility optimization services, M+W Group is providing the infrastructure that keeps the Capital Region at the forefront of nanotechnology research and electronics manufacturing.

Its work includes major facilities for UAlbany CNSE and GLOBALFOUNDRIES, including the world-leading Fab 8 semiconductor wafer facility. In 2010, M+W Group moved its North American headquarters to the Capital Region, signaling a long-term commitment to the region's high-tech future.

STEP

Saratoga Technology + Energy Park® (STEP), created by New York State Energy Research and Development Authority (NYSERDA), serves leading environmental and clean-energy companies.

TEC-SMART

(Training and Education Center for Semiconductor Manufacturing and Alternative and Renewable Technologies). The training center offers college-level semiconductor industry courses within the Saratoga Technology + Energy Park.

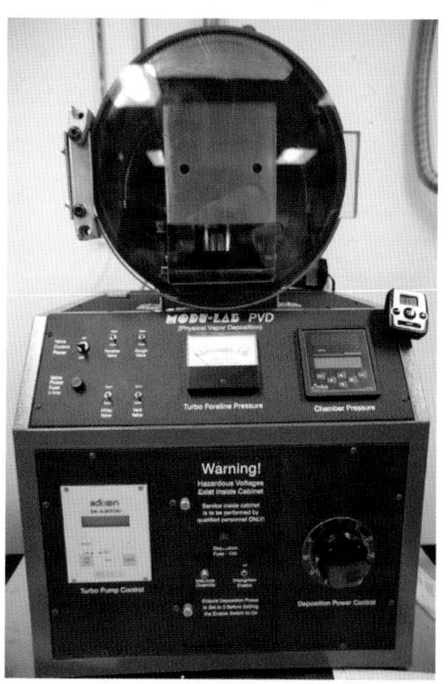

nfrastructure

As one of the top computer information technology companies in the U.S., nfrastructure designs, builds, and maintains computer networks for GLOBALFOUNDRIES, The College of Nanoscale Science & Engineering, and leading U.S. corporations including IBM, Intel, Cisco, Microsoft, HP, Dell and others.

Two data centers in Saratoga County offer redundancy.

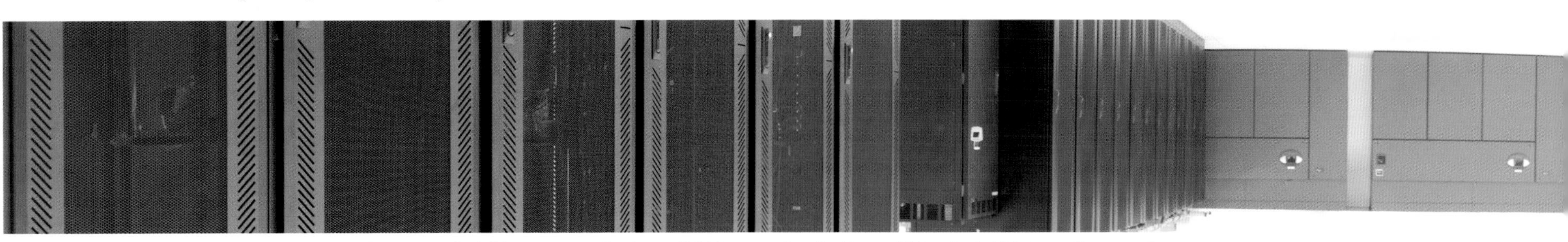

nfrastructure's server room in the Saratoga Technology Park. The company also has a 40,000-square-foot buildng in Clifton Park, NY, also in Saratoga County.

ASML

Based in the Netherlands, with a new office in Saratoga County, ASML provides lithography systems for complex machines that are critical to the production of integrated circuits. ASML delivers advanced systems that help the major chipmakers to reduce the size and increase the functionality of microchips.

Tokyo Electron Ltd.

Tokyo Electron Limited (TEL) is the leading manufacturer of semiconductor production equipment on the planet. TEL develops, manufactures and distributes specialized technologies for the semiconductor production market, including flat panel display (FPD) production equipment. TEL provides leading products and services through a global matrix of approximately 90 locations in 15 countries in North America, Europe, and Asia.

SEMATECH

SEMATECH, the international consortium of leading semiconductor manufacturers, fosters pre-competitive cooperation across the nanoelectronics industry and accelerates the commercialization of technology innovation into manufacturing solutions.

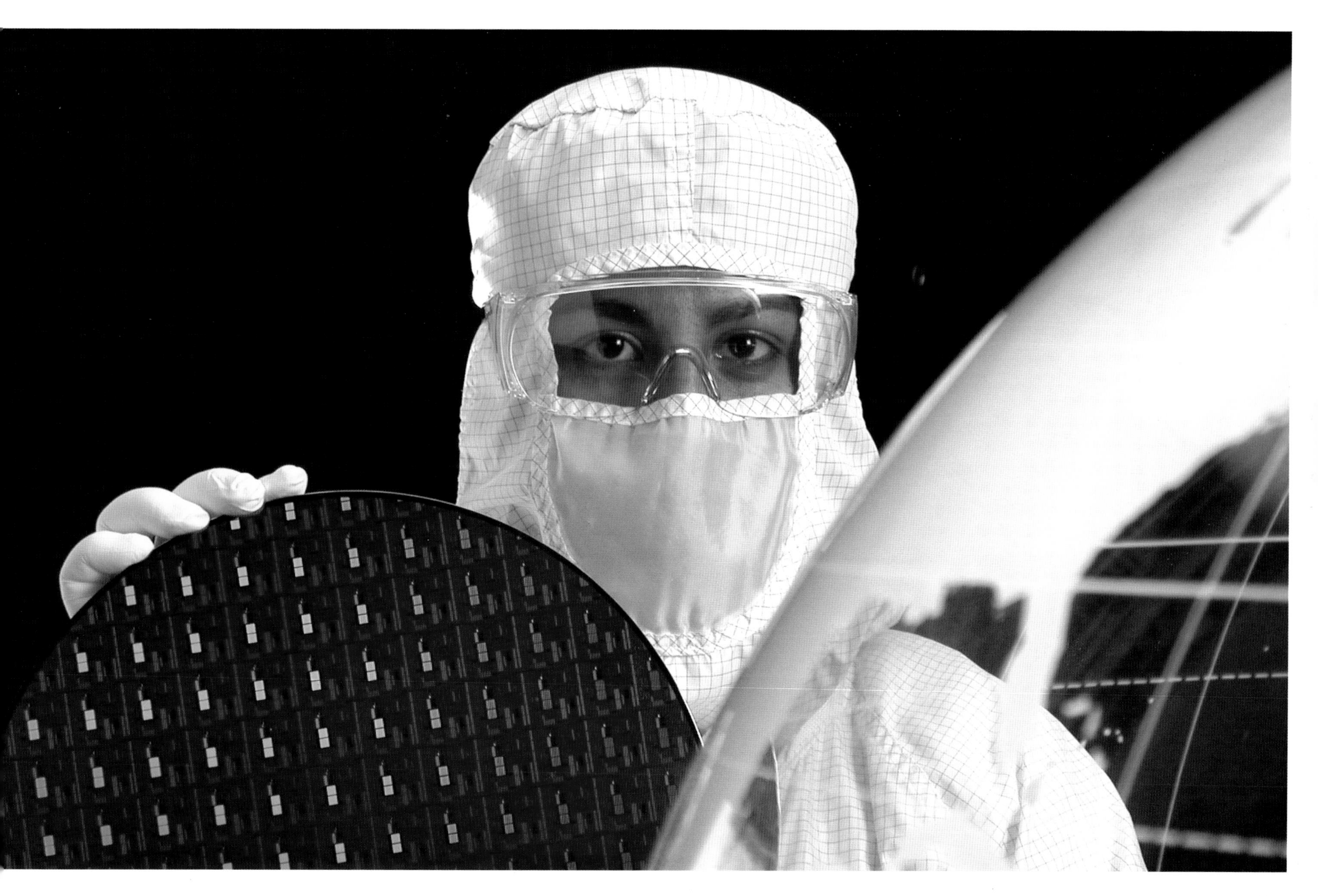

The College of Nanoscale Science & Engineering

The College of Nanoscale Science & Engineering (CNSE) of the University at Albany is the first college in the world dedicated to education, research, development, and deployment in the emerging disciplines of nanoscience, nanoengineering, nanobioscience, and nanoeconomics.

HITACHI
POST
LASER

LEICA
3300

The College of Nanoscale Science & Engineering

CNSE's Albany NanoTech Complex houses the only fully integrated, 300mm wafer, computer chip pilot prototyping and demonstration line, with 80,000 square feet of Class I capable cleanrooms. More than 2,500 scientists, researchers, engineers, students, and faculty work on site, from companies including IBM, GLOBALFOUNDRIES, SEMATECH, Intel, Toshiba, Samsung, Applied Materials, Tokyo Electron, ASML, Novellus Systems, Vistec Lithography, and Atotech.

CNSE has generated over $7.5 billion in public and private investments, including more than $6.5 billion from the international nanoelectronics industry.

The College of Nanoscale Science & Engineering

An expansion now underway is projected to increase the size of CNSE's Albany NanoTech Complex to over 1,250,000 square feet of next-generation infrastructure housing over 135,000 square feet of Class I capable cleanrooms and more than 3,750 scientists, researchers, and engineers from CNSE and global corporations.

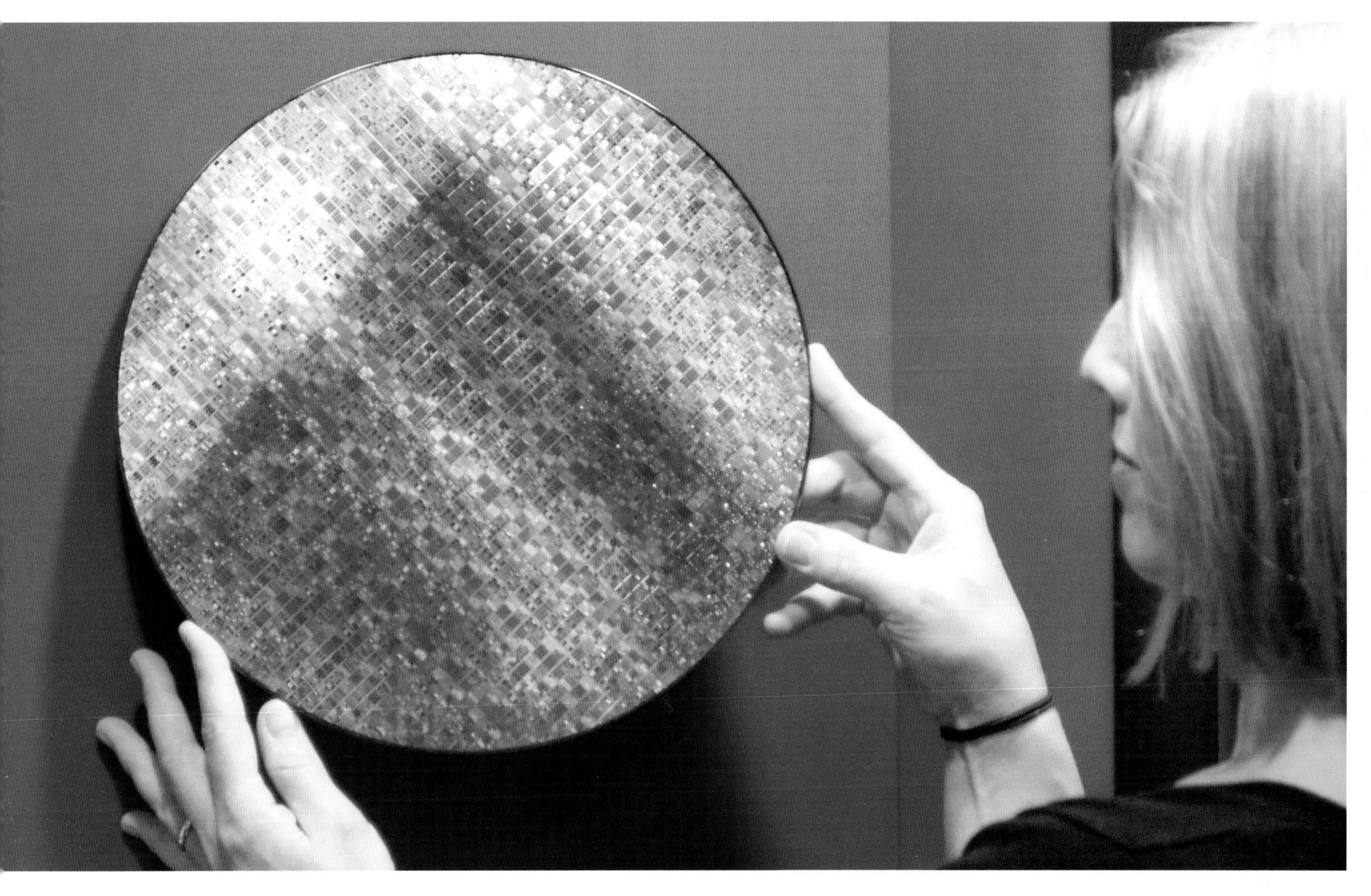

The College of Nanoscale Science & Engineering

The powerful combination of CNSE, IBM, GLOBALFOUNDRIES, and the world's leading nanoelectronics companies makes the region an international destination for cutting-edge research and manufacturing.

GLOBALFOUNDRIES

GLOBALFOUNDRIES is constructing the most technologically advanced semiconductor manufacturing facility in the world and the largest leading-edge semiconductor foundry in the United States, called Fab 8. With additional foundries in Germany and Singapore, GLOBALFOUNDRIES is the world's first truly global semiconductor foundry.

GLOBALFOUNDRIES

The Integrated Technology Development Center (ITDC) is used to test and develop the specialized Automated Materials Handling System (AMHS) prior to installation in the cleanroom.

GLOBALFOUNDRIES

The AMHS is an overhead track that transports, stores, and manages semiconductor wafer carriers during production.

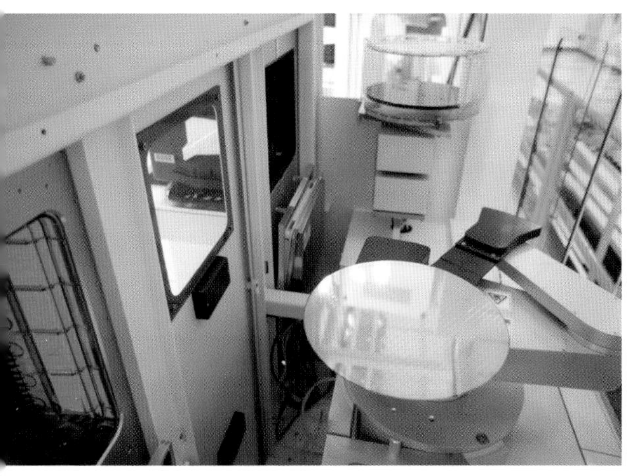

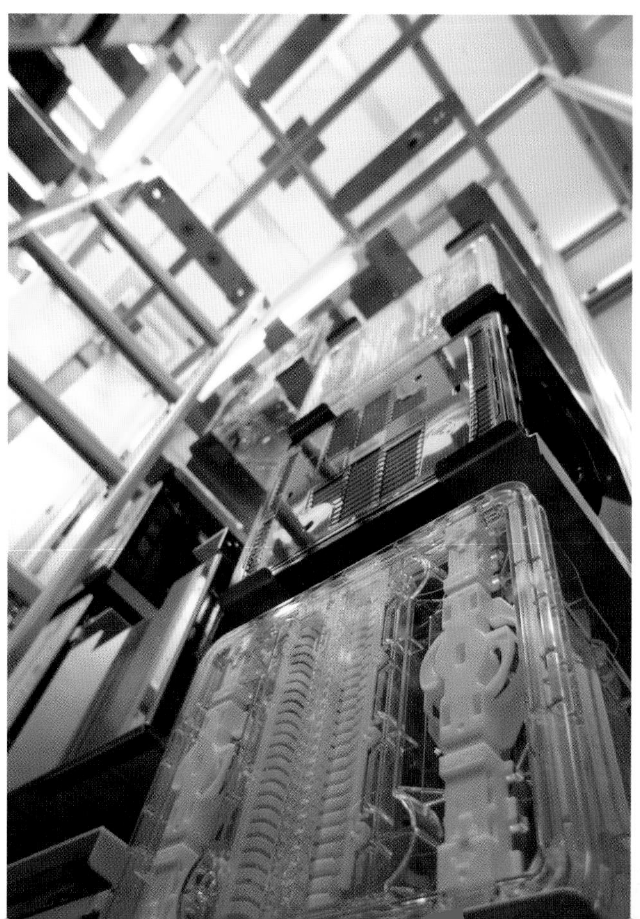

GLOBALFOUNDRIES

The cleanroom size is equivalent to about six football fields – more than the total square footage of the Chrysler Building.

GLOBALFOUNDRIES

The 100-inch stainless ductwork filters and completely recirculates the air within the 300,000-square-foot cleanroom every three minutes.

GLOBALFOUNDRIES

Nine holding tanks supply the millions of gallons of ultra-purified water required to manufacture semiconductor wafers.

GLOBALFOUNDRIES

GLOBALFOUNDRIES initially broke ground on 210,000 square feet of cleanroom space in June 2009. Due to high customer demand, the company decided in 2010 to expand the cleanroom by 90,000 square feet, bringing its total size to 300,000 square feet.

GLOBALFOUNDRIES began construction on a second administration building on June 30, 2011. A major construction project in itself, the Admin 2 building represents a significant addition to the Fab 8 campus and a major new investment in the upstate New York economy.

GLOBALFOUNDRIES

Fab 8 is located on 222 acres in the Luther Forest Technology Campus in Saratoga County, adjacent to Saratoga Lake.

Saratoga: Location, Location, Location

Saratoga is three hours from three of the world's greatest cities, and a half hour from one of the greatest forests. It is located at the crossroads of the New York State Thruway and Route 87, and two-thirds of the U.S. population is within a six-hour drive.

left: The Albany International Airport is twenty-five miles from Saratoga with direct access on a major interstate.

above: North American Flight Services is located at the Saratoga Airport.

below: The new train station easily connects to New York City, Boston, and Montreal.

SARATOGA

HEALTH HISTORY HORSES HI-TECH

Peter Olsen worked as a photographer in New York City prior to working as the senior copywriter on the Nabisco, Nissan, Minolta, Seagram's, and R.J. Reynolds accounts at the William Esty Company in Manhattan. With three children, he and his wife moved to Saratoga for the school system. Olsen Advertising has served numerous tech-startup companies in the Capital Region, with three reaching "The INC 100 List of the Fastest Growing Companies in America." He served five divisions of GE Power Systems, and currently serves companies in the tech sector in Saratoga.

Photography notes.
Most pictures were taken with Sony digital cameras, using Carl Zeiss, Sony, and Minolta lenses. Some were shot with a compact Fuji camera, and some with a 1960s 35mm Nikon FTN. Many photos utilized Sony's High Dynamic Range program.

Editing.
Relentless persistence by Angie Jabine.

Gratitude.
Great thanks to Prof. James Kettlewell, the history department at the Saratoga Springs Public Library, City Historian Mary Ann Fitzgerald, the Saratoga Springs History Museum, Hollis Palmer, Minnie Bolster, Stanton Williamson, Robert A. Moeser, John Leman, GLOBALFOUNDRIES, and The College of Nanoscale Science & Engineering.